DEVILISHNESS

DEVILISHNESS

RIUS

American Atheist Press Austin, TX 1987

copyright page

Originally published as Diabluras: un libro de todos los diablos
in October 1982.

American Atheist Press, P O Box 2117, Austin, TX 78768-2117

Published 1987.
Printed in the United States of America

ISBN: 0-910309-50-7

Heaven

Papini
The Devil

Heaven
No Blacks
No Indians
God's transparent, boy!

THE EXORCIST
The Exorcist

Geometry

Sell your soul? It's not even worth a down payment, Gramps!

That's all I'm going to pay for your soul! Take it or leave it.

You're wasting Your time! God's gay.

Me, disgusting? What kind of proposition did you expect from me?

Commission! What commission?

Would you like to be my guardian angel?

No! Neither Hitler, nor Stalin nor Somoza are here. This is a decent hotel!

I already said, "No!" It must be a false alarm.
Hades

Air
Conditioning
Inc.

HOLY BIBLE
Bible

They called me a son of a bitch!

Doctor
Veterinarian

We came to collect our royalties, honey.

Going down?
No, going up!

There's something I don't like about your lifeline.

It's a birth defect.

And I don't think he's as young as he says he is . . .

Wow! Souls are still going down!
THE JOURNAL
FINANCE

And where did you come from?

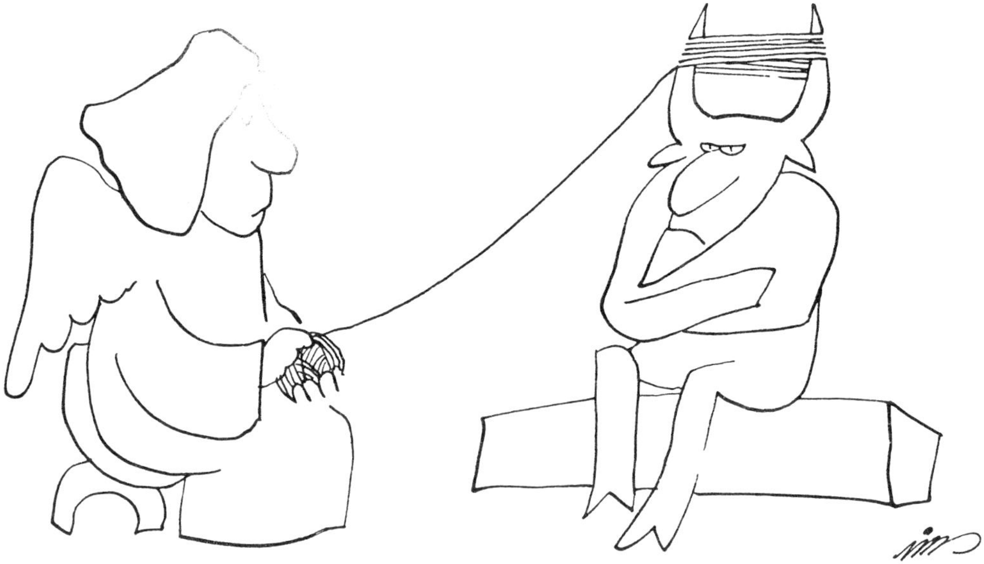

If you don't go to sleep the angels will get you!!

I'm sorry but you're not registered here.

Great, You even scared me!

MISS
LULU
SEX!
She's one of our best agents. .

I imagine he's going back to Spain . . .

unemployment
compensation

Some public relations guy convinced me we had to improve our image . . .

You knew you should stay away from daycare centers!

And do you get paid overtiime?

Your problem is simple. You didn't have a mother.

And please don't go around saying we're related . . .

The poor devil. .

I don't know. I'm not from around here either.

What the devil am I going to do today?

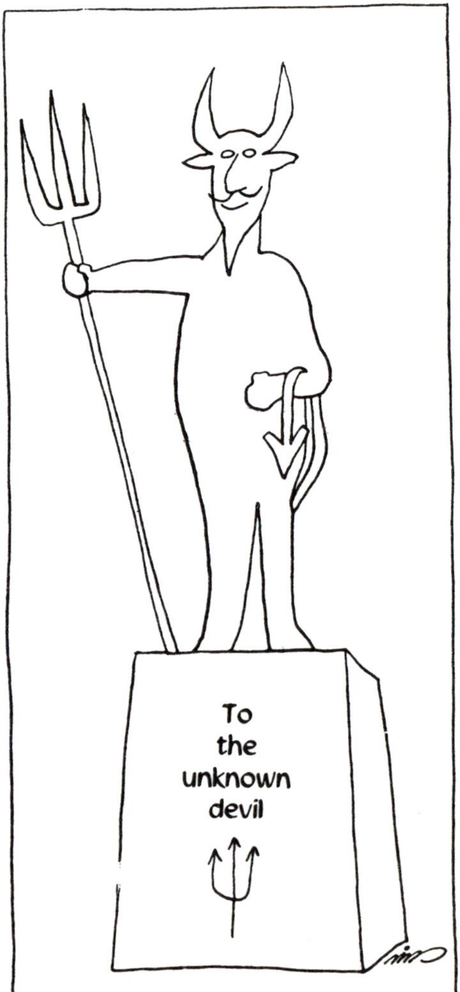
To
the
unknown
devil

Maybe God jinxed you.

Just tell us which Communist Party cell you belong to . . .

Note to foreign readers: In Mexico these dollies are called "Devils."

No! Our best weather is in June and July!

Excuse me, but we forgot our corkscrew.

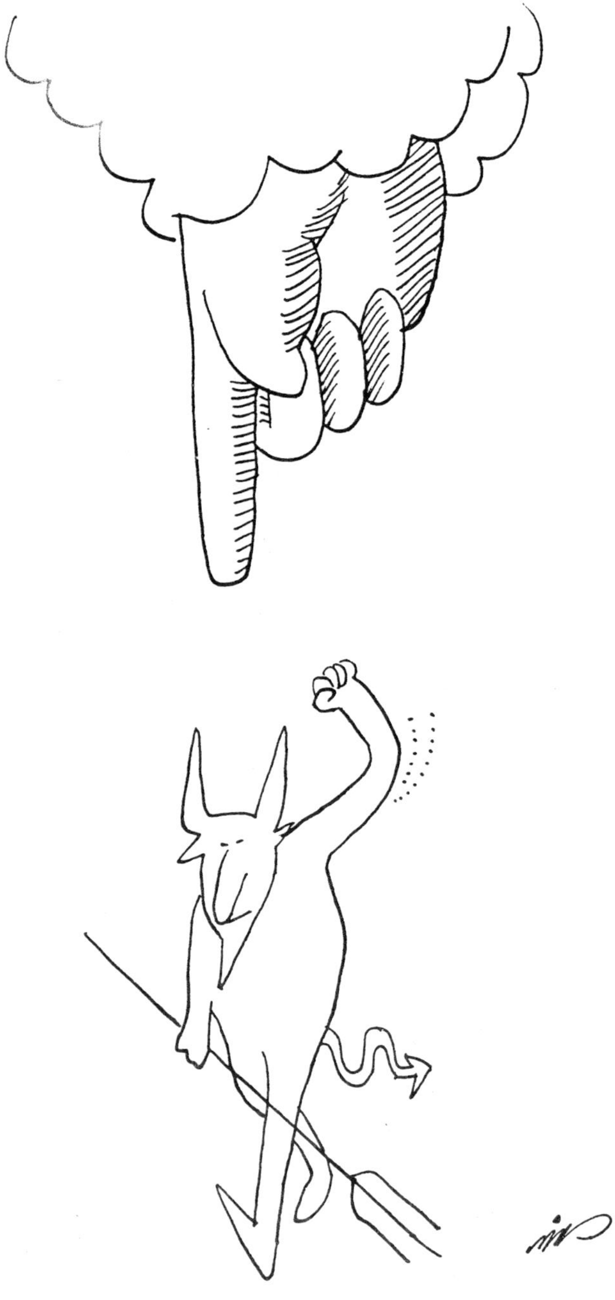

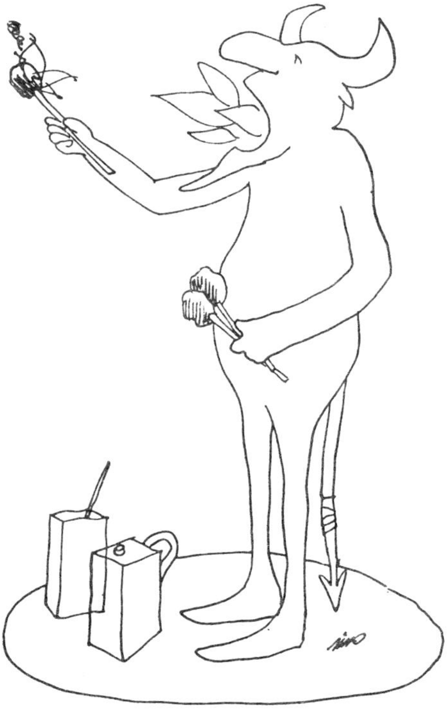

"AIMS AND PURPOSES"

(as recorded in documents of incorporation)

AMERICAN ATHEISTS ARE ORGANIZED:

(1) to stimulate and promote freedom of thought and inquiry concerning religious beliefs, creeds, dogmas, tenets, rituals, and practices;

(2) to collect and disseminate information, data, and literature on all religions and promote a more thorough understanding of them, their origins, and their histories;

(3) to advocate, labor for, and promote in all lawful ways the complete and absolute separation of state and church;

(4) to advocate, labor for, and promote in all lawful ways the establishment and maintenance of a thoroughly secular system of education available to all;

(5) to encourage the development and public acceptance of a humane ethical system, stressing the mutual sympathy, understanding, and interdependence of all people and the corresponding responsibility of each individual in relation to society;

(6) to develop and propagate a social philosophy in which man is the central figure, who alone must be the source of strength, progress, and ideals for the well-being and happiness of humanity;

(7) to promote the study of the arts and sciences and of all problems affecting the maintenance, perpetuation, and enrichment of human (and other) life; and

(8) to engage in such social, educational, legal, and cultural activity as will be useful and beneficial to members of American Atheists and to society as a whole.

"DEFINITIONS"

Atheism is the *Weltanschauung* (comprehensive conception of the world and of total human life value systems) of persons who are *free* from theism — *i.e.,* free *from* religion. It is predicated on ancient Greek Materialism.

American Atheism may be defined as the mental attitude that unreservedly accepts the supremacy of reason and aims at establishing a life-style and ethical outlook verifiable by experience and the scientific method, independent of all arbitrary assumptions of authority or creeds.

Materialism declares that the cosmos is devoid of immanent conscious purpose; that it is governed by its own inherent, immutable, and impersonal laws; that there is no supernatural interference in human life; that man — finding his resources within himself — can and must create his own destiny. Materialism restores to man his dignity and his intellectual integrity. It teaches that we must prize our life on earth and strive always to improve it. It holds that man is capable of creating a social system based on reason and justice. Materialism's "faith" is in man and man's ability to transform the world culture by his own efforts. This is a commitment which is in every essence life-asserting. It considers the struggle for progress as a moral obligation and impossible without noble ideas that inspire man to struggle and bold creative works. Materialism holds that humankind's potential for good and for an outreach to more fulfilling cultural development is, for all practical purposes, unlimited.

American Atheists is a nonpolitical, nonprofit, educational organization. Another of its functions is to act as a "watchdog" to challenge any attempted breach of what Thomas Jefferson called "the wall of separation between state and church," upon which principle our nation was founded.

Membership is open only to those who are in accord with the "Aims and Purposes" indicated above and who are Atheist Materialists. Membership in the national organization is a prerequisite for membership in state, county, city, or local chapters. Membership fee categories are reflected on the reverse side of this sheet (American Atheists Membership Application form).

A complete copy of the Constitution and By-Laws of American Atheists is available upon request. Send $1.00 for postage and handling to:

Constitution and By-Laws
American Atheists, Inc.
P.O. Box 2117
Austin, TX 78768-2117

Membership Application For American Atheists

Last name: ______________________ First name: ______________________

Companion's name (if family or couple membership)

Last name: ______________________ First name: ______________________

Address ____

City/State/Zip ____

This is to certify that I am/we are in agreement with the "Aims and Purposes"* and the "Definitions"* of American Atheists. I/we consider myself/ourselves to be Materialist or Non-theist (*i.e.*, A-theist) and I/we have, therefore, a particular interest in the separation of state and church and American Atheists' efforts on behalf of that principle.

I/we usually identify myself/ourselves for public purposes as (check one):

☐ Atheist	☐ Objectivist	☐ Agnostic
☐ Freethinker	☐ Ethical Culturalist	☐ Realist
☐ Humanist	☐ Unitarian	☐ I/we evade any reply to a query
☐ Rationalist	☐ Secularist	

☐ Other: ____

I am/we are, however, an Atheist(s) and I/we hereby make application for membership in American Atheists. Both dues and contributions are to a tax-exempt organization and I/we may claim these amounts as tax deductions on my/our income tax return(s). *(This application must be dated and signed by the applicant(s) to be accepted.)*

Signature ______________________________ Date ______________

Signature ______________________________ Date ______________

Membership in American Atheists includes a subscription to the monthly journal *American Atheist* and the monthly "Insider's Newsletter" as well as all the other rights and privileges of membership. Please indicate your choice of membership dues:

☐ Life, $500	☐ Individual, $40/year
☐ Couple Life, $750 (Please give both names above.)	☐ Age 65 or over, $20/year (Photocopy of ID required.)
☐ Sustaining, $100/year	☐ Unemployed, $20/year
☐ Couple/Family, $50/year (Please give all names above.)	☐ Student, $12/year (Photocopy of ID required.)

Upon your acceptance into membership, you will receive a handsome gold embossed membership card, a membership certificate personally signed by Jon G. Murray, president of American Atheists, our special monthly "Insider's Newsletter" to keep you informed of the activities of American Atheists, and a subscription to *American Atheist*. Life members receive a specially embossed pen and pencil set; sustaining members receive a commemorative pen. Your name will be sent to the chapter in your local area if there currently is one, and you will be contacted so you may become a part of the many local activities. Memberships and subscriptions are nonrefundable.

☐ I am/we are enclosing a check or money order for $ ____________ payable to: American Atheists

☐ Please charge my/our charge card for $ ________. ☐ Visa or ☐ Mastercard

Card # ____

Bank No./Letters ____

Expiration date: ____

Signature ____

Return form to:

American Atheists, Inc., P.O. Box 2117, Austin, TX 78768-2117

Don't Miss The *American Atheist*

Founded by the first lady of Atheism, Dr. Madalyn O'Hair, the *American Atheist* is the magazine of the modern Atheist.

From the latest deeds of Atheist activists to the last antics of the religious right, its articles run the gamut of issues important to Atheists. Skirmishes in the state/church separation battle, the life-style and history of Atheism, religious criticism, current events are all included in the focus of this journal. The nation's hottest topics — school prayer, abortion, creationism — are all covered in its pages from the Atheist's viewpoint.

This magazine's writers bring readers a unique spectrum of viewpoints from literally all over the world. Examples? One columnist offers glimpses into the religions of India. Another highlights the pain of women in the Arab world. Jon Murray, president of American Atheists, spotlights the progress of Atheism (and religion) in the United States.

So why miss any more of this fascinating magazine? Though it is free to members of American Atheists, it is also available to nonmembers on a yearly subscription basis. Go ahead: Check off a box below and head into the wonderful world of Atheism.

☐ Regular subscription, $25
☐ Foreign subscription, $35
☐ Sustaining subscription, $50 (tax-deductable)
☐ Sample copy, $2

Last name: ____________________ First name: ____________________

Address: ____

City/State/Zip: ____

☐ I am enclosing a check or money order for $ __________ payable to American Atheists.

☐ Please charge my credit card for $ __________. ☐ Visa or ☐ Mastercard

Card # ____

Bank No./Letters ________________________________

Expiration date: ________________________________

Signature ____

Return form to:
American Atheists, Inc., P.O. Box 2117, Austin, TX 78768-2117